THE
TARKA AND DARTMOOR
LINES

· A PAST and PRESENT COMPANION ·

SOUTHERN RAILWAY.

(12/28)   (787)

FROM WATERLOO TO

BARNSTAPLE JUNC.

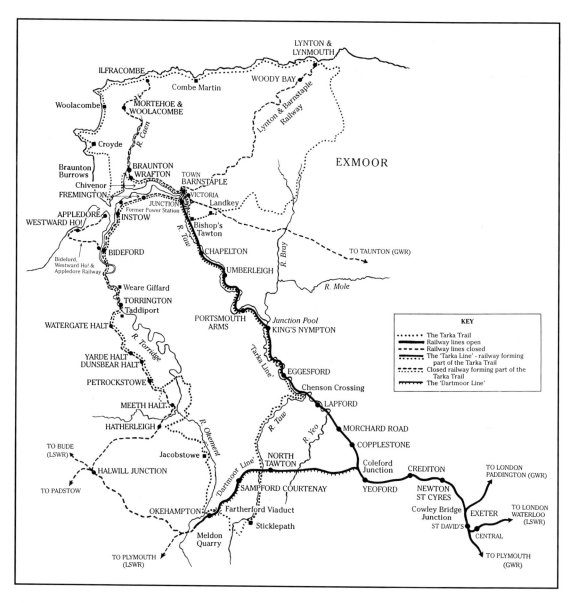

Map of the Tarka Trail, showing the Tarka Line from Exeter to Barnstaple and the Dartmoor Line to Okehampton.

THE
TARKA AND DARTMOOR LINES

· A PAST and PRESENT COMPANION ·

A nostalgic journey by train from Exeter to Barnstaple and Okehampton

Terry Gough

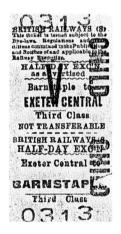

· RAILWAY HERITAGE ·
from
The NOSTALGIA Collection

First published in June 1998

British Library Cataloguing in Publication Data

A catalogue record for this book is available from the British Library.

ISBN 1 85895 139 9

Past & Present Publishing Ltd
The Trundle
Ringstead Road
Great Addington
Kettering
Northamptonshire NN14 4BW

Maps drawn by Christina Siviter

Some of the material in this book first appeared in *British Railways Past and Present Special: The Tarka Trail*, published by Past & Present in 1995.

Printed and bound in Great Britain

Past and Present

A Past & Present book
from
The NOSTALGIA *Collection*

Title page The author was issued with this traditional pre-printed card ticket on his first visit to the Tarka Line on 6 September 1953. In the early 1980s these began to be replaced by a variety of tickets with destinations printed on demand. The BR ticket for the same journey was issued almost exactly 40 years after the first.

CONTENTS

Introduction and acknowledgements   7

The approach to North Devon:
     Exeter Central and St David's   9
Exeter to Yeoford   16
Coleford Junction to Barnstaple Junction   23
Coleford Junction to Okehampton and Meldon Quarry   74

Bibliography   95
Index of locations   96

Author's collection

In the early days of diesel operation, trains displayed a headcode, of little value to passengers but intended to inform railway staff. Here '2C79' signifies the type of train (2), the operating area (C), and the route (79); it is an Ilfracombe train leaving King's Nympton in the summer of 1967.

Present-day King's Nympton from the same point shows a Barnstaple-bound train consisting of Class '153' No 153355 passing through the station on 27 August 1993. *Both TG*

INTRODUCTION

'Among the quiet hills and meadows in the middle of Devon,
this small train of three spruce coaches was the only moving
object, and its harmless racket the only sound.'

from *The Kingdom of the Sea* by Paul Theroux

The Tarka Trail is a long distance path in North Devon completed in 1992, and giving visitors the opportunity to enjoy the area without the intrusion of the motor car. It is centred on Barnstaple, from which it describes a figure of eight, with its extremities at Lynton and Okehampton. Different parts of the Trail can be covered by rail, by foot and by cycle, and in total it covers 180 miles of some of the most beautiful countryside in the United Kingdom.

The various elements of the Trail are not all new, and a significant part makes use of railway lines. Indeed, Barnstaple is reached by train from Exeter, a route named the 'Tarka Line' in 1990, and from Eggesford to Barnstaple the line actually constitutes part of the Trail. Closed railway lines also form part of the Trail, and these are covered in a companion book. This book covers the railway line from Exeter Central to Barnstaple, which has an almost hourly service on weekdays. Also included is the line from Exeter to Okehampton, which has a limited passenger service.

The origins of this book began unwittingly as a result of my first visit to North Devon in 1953, when I set myself the objective of seeing how far I could reach (and return) by rail in one day from my home in Surrey. The destination was Barnstaple, but in this I failed; late running of my train meant that to avoid missing the last train of the day back home, I had to turn round at Umberleigh.

Rail travel in North Devon suffered continuous decline from the late 1950s and resulted in closure of the lines radiating from Barnstaple and the main line across the northern edge of Dartmoor to Okehampton and Plymouth. The Exeter to Barnstaple line survived, and in recent years it has become increasingly popular, in large measure the result of promotion of the line by the Devon and Cornwall Rail Partnership. The North Devon Rail Users Group has also played an important role in ensuring better usage of the line, which currently has a more frequent service than ever before. Unless there is a change in policy and the travelling habits of the public, the future of the Tarka Line is assured. There is even talk of re-introducing freight trains, but as yet there is no practical outcome to this proposal. The possibility of re-opening part of the lines beyond Barnstaple has also been mooted.

In part encouraged by the success of the Tarka Line, pressure has been mounting over the last few years to re-open to passengers the line from Exeter to Okehampton. Support has come from Devon County Council, West Devon Borough Council, Dartmoor National Park and other parties concerned about the ever-increasing number of cars bringing visitors to Dartmoor. The line from the site of Coleford Junction to Meldon Quarry is owned by CAMAS for the carriage of stone traffic; no stone trains run at weekends, so since 1997 it has been possible to run a summer Sunday passenger service between Exeter and Okehampton, the route now being referred to as the 'Dartmoor Line'.

The number of passengers who used the new service in the first year far outnumbered predictions. The service is aimed mainly at those who wish to visit Dartmoor, and all trains connect at Okehampton station with buses to transport visitors to the Moor and beyond. A 'Dartmoor Sunday Rover' ticket is a very cheap way to explore the area. Okehampton station, which lay derelict following the loss of its passenger services in 1972, has been renovated and decorated in 'Southern' style, and there is a visitors' centre including excellent refreshment facilities and a first-class book and model shop. In the former station yard the old goods shed has been converted into a very attractive youth hostel.

Changes are also taking place a few miles further west at Meldon Viaduct. The railway line terminates immediately before the viaduct at Meldon Quarry. The viaduct itself has been out of use since the quarry headshunt was removed. However, it has been fully restored and from 1999 it will gain a new lease of life, this time as part of the Round Devon Cycle Route Network.

It is hoped that the efforts of the last few years by many groups and individuals to make North and West Devon more accessible by public transport will be amply rewarded by increasing numbers of visitors making use of the train.

ACKNOWLEDGEMENTS

I have received much help from Bryony Harris of the North Devon Record Office. I have received support from many photographers, whose names are recorded in the captions. I thank Derek Mercer for expertly printing my negatives. I am grateful to British Rail for lineside access, to CAMAS (and its predecessors) for allowing entry to Meldon Quarry, and to the owners of Eggesford House for allowing entry to their private estate. I am grateful for the interest shown in this edition by Devon County Council and the Tarka Project. My wife has accompanied me on most of the visits to obtain material for this book, a most enjoyable experience for us both.

Terry Gough
Sherborne, Dorset

THE APPROACH TO NORTH DEVON

There were two railway routes to Barnstaple, the Great Western Railway (GWR) line from Taunton, which was opened in 1873, and the London & South Western Railway (LSWR) line from Exeter. The former, which ran through Dulverton and South Molton, had in steam days a bi-hourly service; there were also several through trains from London (Paddington) on summer Saturdays. The decline of the line began in the late 1950s, and towards the end of its life services were reduced to a handful of local trains. The GWR station at Barnstaple closed to passengers in 1960 and trains were diverted to the ex-LSWR station at Barnstaple Junction, then the line from Taunton closed completely in 1966. Present-day motorists, the majority unwittingly, follow the course of this line for much of its route, by virtue of approaching Barnstaple along the North Devon Link Road.

The LSWR line to Barnstaple has a complex history, which is well recorded in a number of books (see the Bibliography). Trains ran regularly from Waterloo to Exeter Queen Street (later renamed Central), and points further west. In summer months many of these trains were packed to capacity with holidaymakers, and on Saturdays additional trains were provided. The fall in the number of railway passengers from the late 1950s also had a dramatic effect on these services, so that by the time the use of steam traction was coming to an end, so were the through services from London to North Devon. The last regular through trains from Waterloo ran in the summer of 1964. The complete abandonment of all North Devon lines and the ex-LSWR main line to Plymouth became a serious consideration. In the event the North Devon line is still open for passengers as far as Barnstaple (the 'Tarka Line') and the Plymouth line as far as Meldon Quarry (just beyond Okehampton) for stone trains. There is also a Sunday passenger service to Okehampton. There are still services from both Paddington and Waterloo to Exeter, with the former being the quicker and giving much better connections at Exeter St David's for the Barnstaple trains.

However, the line from Waterloo is both the historically 'correct' way to connect with Barnstaple and Okehampton trains, and is by far the more scenically attractive route, passing over Salisbury Plain, along the Blackmoor Vale and through a succession of junction stations that used to serve branches to Dorset and East Devon towns, of which only the Exmouth branch survives. The LSWR main line has been managed successively by the Southern Railway, and the Southern and (west of Salisbury) the Western Regions of British Rail. It more recently became part of Network SouthEast and, from April 1994, has been operated by South West Trains.

Steam-hauled 12-coach trains from Waterloo to Exeter were once commonplace, but they gave way to shorter and shorter diesel locomotive-hauled trains as the railway lost its passengers

London and South Western Ry.

787

TO

EXETER (QUEEN ST.)

SOUTHERN RAILWAY.

(1/34)   (787)

FROM WATERLOO TO

EXETER CENTRAL

Author's collection

to road transport. The increasing migration of holidaymakers to other European countries also played a significant part. The line declined in importance and could well have closed, had it not been for a change in policy within railway management and pressure from communities along the route to revitalise it. Several stations between Salisbury and Exeter, closed in the 1960s, have been reopened and the service has been much improved in the last few years. In 1993 new trains were introduced on all Waterloo to Exeter services, and further improvements in frequency were made in 1994, so the old LSWR line remains an ideal route by which to reach the Tarka and Dartmoor Lines.

The present-day visitor arriving at Exeter Central will be struck by the size of the station in comparison to its services. It was opened by the Southern Railway in 1933 on the site of the LSWR Queen Street station, and was the point at which many of the express trains from London were divided, with parts for North Devon, North Cornwall and Plymouth. It was also the starting point for many local trains heading both east and west. The branch line trains to Exmouth also started here. There was a local goods yard and carriage sidings

adjacent to the station, as well as much larger yards and engine sheds at Exmouth Junction 1¼ miles to the east.

The station buildings remain superficially unchanged, although much has been let for non-railway use, the track layout has been simplified and the goods yard and carriage sidings closed. Trains no longer divide here and services from Waterloo mostly continue only as far as the next station at Exeter St David's. The Exmouth branch trains still run and a very frequent service is provided; in addition there are a few

What a welcome to the West Country! This is the 'Atlantic Coast Express' from Waterloo arriving at Exeter Central station during a downpour in midsummer 1960. The engine is 'West Country' Class No 34108 *Wincanton*, built by British Railways in 1950 to a Southern Railway design. The following year this engine was rebuilt and its streamlined casing removed to give a more conventional appearance. The engine to the right has just arrived with a train from Exmouth.

The new image is represented by a South Western Turbo train of Class '159', which were introduced exclusively for the Waterloo and Exeter services in 1993 to replace ageing diesel locomotives and coaches. This is No 159015 on the 12.35 from Waterloo on 5 September 1994. *Both TG*

morning and evening local trains that run to Honiton and Yeovil Junction. There are, of course, also the Tarka Line trains operated by Wales & West, which start either here or come from Exmouth.

The line between Exeter Queen St and Exeter St David's was opened in 1862. Immediately beyond the western end of the LSWR station the railway line makes one of the steepest descents of a main line in the country at a gradient of 1 in 37, made more challenging by incorporating a tunnel and a very tight curve, culminating in the junction with the GWR main line at St David's. A day spent at this location in steam days was fascinating, as a succession of trains tackled the bank.

The 2.21 pm Exeter Central to Barnstaple and Torrington train descends to St David's behind 'Battle of Britain' Class No 34110 *66 Squadron* on 12 August 1960. Climbing the bank is sister engine No 34074 *46 Squadron* on the 2.20 pm from Ilfracombe, which will form the rear portion of the 4.30 pm from Exeter Central to Waterloo.

The front portion, from Plymouth and Padstow, is already in the station. The stock in the carriage siding will form a slow train to Salisbury. There are other carriage sidings to the right, and the station is immediately beyond the road bridge; the end of the down platform is just visible.

By 3 April 1986 the carriage sidings have made way for a builders' merchant, as a Barnstaple-bound train consisting of just three coaches descends to St David's. The first-generation BR diesel multiple units (DMUs) were used on most local trains in the West of England. *Both TG*

Watching a train climb the bank was impressive both to see and hear, particularly as it burst into the open from the tunnel. The heavier trains had at least one banking engine attached to the rear for the ascent and sometimes a second engine on the front as well. The heaviest trains were those conveying stone from Meldon Quarry near Okehampton, and on 12 August 1960 one such train was hauled by BR Standard Class '3MT' No 82025 and Class 'N' No 31844.

Meldon Quarry is still open, but stone trains no longer use this route to South East England, but reverse at Exeter Riverside yard (near St David's) and use the former GWR line. The Waterloo trains still pound up the bank, however, although to a very different sound; that emitted by the diesel engine. Until 1993 all Waterloo trains were hauled by diesel locomotives, such as this Class '50', No 50017 *Royal Oak*, which is working the 12.20 to Waterloo in the summer of 1986. *Both TG*

On emerging from the western end of the tunnel the rail traveller is treated to a rooftop view of the houses in Bonhay Road and the River Exe beyond. The present St David's station is the third on this site and was built by the GWR in 1914. It is almost unique in that trains from London regularly arrive from opposite directions; the only other example in the South West was Plymouth North Road until the closure of the LSWR route via Okehampton. Another feature is the sight of two trains leaving from the same platform almost simultaneously in opposite directions.

'T9' Class locomotives were often used on secondary trains to Okehampton and beyond. The last time the author travelled behind one of these engines was on 11 August 1960, when No 30729 worked the 3.13 pm from Padstow to Exeter Central. It is seen here at St David's waiting to tackle the bank.

Dual occupancy of Platform 1 on 26 May 1987. Class '142' railbus No 142019 has just arrived on the 11.45 from Exmouth, to trap the 12.18 to Waterloo hauled by Class '50' No 50040 *Centurion*. The Barnstaple train in Platform 3 will also leave at 12.18, and is formed of another of the Class '142' railbuses known as 'Skippers', introduced amidst great publicity a few months earlier. Unfortunately the rigid wheelbase of these vehicles made them unsuitable for some of the lines in Devon and Cornwall and they were transferred away from the area in September 1987. In the intervening period the ageing diesel units introduced at the end of the steam era had been withdrawn for scrap, and for many months following the departure of the '142s' Tarka Line trains were worked by an assortment of diesel units or locomotives borrowed from other parts of the British Rail network.

This collection of old diesel units was not replaced until 1992 when new-generation units of Class '150' and others of similar design were allocated to all Devon and Cornwall branch lines. On 30 April 1994 platform 1 at St David's is occupied by Class '150' No 150230 forming a Paignton train. Behind is No 150269, recently arrived from Barnstaple, and on the left is Class '159' No 159005 leaving for the sidings after working the 10.35 from Waterloo. *All TG*

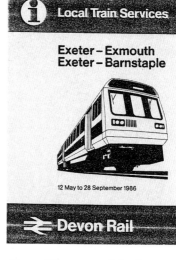

Above **The cover of the Summer 1986 timetable.** *Author's collection*

EXETER TO YEOFORD

Immediately after leaving Exeter St David's trains pass the extensive freight yards of Exeter Riverside, where ballast wagons used on the stone trains from Meldon Quarry are often to be seen. Cowley Bridge, at the end of the yard, was the junction of the LSWR lines to Plymouth and Ilfracombe, and the GWR line to Bristol and beyond. Both railway companies used the same tracks between St David's and Cowley Bridge; plans for separate lines for each company never materialised. Cowley Bridge Junction still exists, but in simplified form, with the ex-LSWR line now being single track. Cowley Bridge also marks the confluence of the Rivers Exe and Yeo.

The line climbs gently beyond Cowley Bridge and passes through the stations of Newton St Cyres and Crediton. The latter town is worth a visit, and although not particularly attractive, with a main road passing through the centre, is of historical significance and was diocesan home of the bishop until this was transferred to Exeter in the 11th century.

Beyond Crediton the line climbs more steadily to Yeoford. The valley is still wide here as the river meanders from one side of the railway to the other. The Crediton to Barnstaple and Fremington line was opened three years after the Exeter to Crediton section, and was provided with broad gauge services until 1877. From 1863 standard gauge trains also ran between Exeter and Bideford. Through services between Exeter and Fremington began in 1855.

Right **A 1980s poster advertising the railways of Devon. At that time the Barnstaple line was still referred to by its traditional name of the North Devon Line.** *TG*

Below **The line between Exeter St David's and Crediton was opened in 1851 and broad gauge trains were provided until 1892. A Barnstaple-bound train crosses the River Exe just beyond Cowley Bridge on 18 August 1989 and gives the traveller the first indications of the beauty of the countryside ahead.** *TG*

Newton St Cyres has always been served only by local trains, the expresses passing through en route to Plymouth and Ilfracombe. The first view shows the station in the late 1960s, looking towards Yeoford.

Today the station is served by a small number of the 'Tarka Line' trains on request to the guard or by flagging down if one wishes to board. Several other stations on the 'Tarka Line' are served in this way, which is an admirable method of retaining a station that generates little revenue but performs a valuable social function. The double track has been removed and the down platform abandoned. Unit 829 leaves with a Barnstaple service in October 1990. *Both TG*

The third view is looking towards Exeter on 24 August 1989, with a Barnstaple train approaching the station. According to the winter 1993/4 timetable Newton St Cyres was in the unique position of having a Saturday-only train start here 'by request' and running as far as Umberleigh. A more careful study of the timetable revealed that the journey time from Newton St Cyres to Crediton was 42 minutes and to Umberleigh only 1 minute. British Rail subsequently issued an amendment claiming that this service was now discontinued, rather than admitting to misprints. *TG*

Below left Many of the 'Tarka Line' trains pass each other at Crediton, which is also the terminus for some trains from Exeter that run as part of a 'Park and Ride' scheme introduced in 1992. The old station buildings survive, although there are no booking facilities. The LSWR signal box at the west end of the station is still in use, controlling the barriers that have long since replaced the traditional railway level crossing gates. It is here that the drivers of Barnstaple-bound trains are given authority to proceed on the single line to the next passing place at Eggesford. This is undertaken manually using a modern version of the railway 'token'. Above is a view of Crediton from an Exeter-bound train on 3 August 1991, with Unit No 879 waiting clearance to leave for Barnstaple. This unit was made up from odd coaches of Classes '101' and '108' subsequent to the withdrawal of the 'Skippers'.

In 1997 an Okehampton-bound train, consisting of unit No 150248, stands at Crediton during the first summer season of the re-instated passenger service from Exeter. *Both TG*

The view from the footbridge at the west end of Crediton clearly shows two tracks, but these are operated as completely separate lines; the old down line is used exclusively by trains to and from Okehampton and Meldon Quarry, while all 'Tarka Line' trains use the old up line, hence the need for single line 'token' operation. There are several stone trains per day with corresponding return empty wagon workings. The times are variable, but there is usually one in each direction mid-morning, which together with the passenger trains to and from Exeter makes Crediton busy for short periods. These two 12 August 1988 photographs show Class '33' No 33039 approaching the station with a stone train (above), and a down empty stone train leaving Crediton hauled by Class '50' No 50042. *Both TG*

SOUTHERN RAILWAY.

(1/82)

TO

Stock 787

YEOFORD JUNCTION

Author's collection

Yeoford, although serving a small community, was a busy interchange station until the end of the steam era. There were extensive sidings and much traffic in cattle, agricultural produce and equipment. A visit on a dismal day in August 1960 found both passenger and freight activity. 'West Country' Class No 34002 *Salisbury* approaches the station on the 11.47 am Exeter Central to Plymouth, while 'Battle of Britain' Class No 34056 *Croydon*, on an up freight train, waits in the bay.

All this has since been swept aside, as the same view in the 1980s shows. There are no sidings, no signals and only one platform, but at least the station is still open, although served mostly on request. The train is unit No P471 of Class '118' forming the 14.30 Barnstaple to Exeter St David's service. *Both TG*

The extent of the passenger facilities at Yeoford can be judged by this 1960 view of the station. In the 'present' photograph a Barnstaple to Exeter train formed of unit No 150241 passes the overgrown old down platform and yard on 7 September 1994. *Both TG*

'Battle of Britain' Class No 34056 *Croydon* works an up freight train into Yeoford on 11 August 1960. The train will set back into the siding on the right to allow an express passenger train to pass (see page 20).

    Another freight train, this time of stone from Meldon Quarry, is seen on 7 September 1994 immediately on the other side of the bridge by Yeoford station. The engine is Class '37' No 37191, which had taken empties to Meldon about 2 hours earlier. *Both TG*

COLEFORD JUNCTION TO BARNSTAPLE JUNCTION

The lines to Okehampton and Barnstaple diverged 1 mile beyond Yeoford at Coleford Junction, the former continuing west and the latter turning north-west. The first sod of the line from Yeoford to Okehampton was cut by the Countess of Portsmouth near here in 1864. A narrow road from Coleford village passes over the railway just west of the junction and gives good views of both lines, although foliage blocks the view of the 'Tarka Line' during the summer months. The junction was taken out in 1971, the two lines now running parallel to the junction at Crediton.

Copplestone is situated at the junction of the main roads to Barnstaple (A377) and Okehampton (A3072), and is the highest point on the railway from Exeter; hereafter the line falls all the way to Barnstaple. As the line approaches Copplestone it enters a cutting sandwiched between the northbound and southbound sections of the A377, here occupied by an afternoon Exeter to Barnstaple train in August 1988 consisting of unit No 956 of Class '108'. Copplestone has a place in railway history because it was in this cutting that the first sod of the North Devon Railway was cut in 1852 by the Hon Newton Fellowes, who became 4th Earl of Portsmouth (see page 36). *TG*

A present-day souvenir platform ticket for Copplestone, issued at Barnstaple, and a luggage label issued by the LSWR. *Both author's collection*

Old and new station signs and an oil lamp at Copplestone. *All TG*

Although engineering works for double track between Copplestone and Umberleigh were undertaken, track was never laid and this section has always been single track with passing loops at intermediate stations. Coleford Junction to Copplestone was doubled in 1883. These are views looking towards Barnstaple before and after 'rationalisation'. The former up platform was taken out of use many years ago, and there is only single track through the station. There has been a further recent change in that the abattoir on the left has been demolished. *Both TG*

Morchard Road station, built to serve the village of Morchard Bishop $2^1/_2$ miles to the north-east, is, like all stations beyond Coleford Junction, close to the main A377 road. This has the advantage of easy access, but suffers from competition from road transport. Here is the station seen from Morchard Road bridge on 7 June 1994; the train is the 09.24 Exmouth to Barnstaple, which stops here by request. In common with most other stations on the line, Morchard Road was oil-lit, but the lamps were removed many years ago. More recently electric light has been installed, tactfully using lamps of the traditional style, although far taller than the originals. Morchard Road had a passing loop until 1964. *TG*

London and South Western Ry.

787

TO

MORCHARD RD.

Author's collection

Between Morchard Road and Lapford, the road and railway are joined by a river, the second River Yeo in the county. The view looking north at this point is most attractive, although the river is hidden from view behind the trees to the right of the railway line. This point also marks the beginning of the meandering of the line to follow the river. Class '155' No 155315 forms an afternoon train from Barnstaple in July 1992. *TG*

Opposite Lapford station is close to the village and at one time the platforms for up and down trains were separated by the Exeter Road overbridge; all trains now use the former up platform. There is also a road bridge a few yards to the south of the station carrying a minor road to the village, and this gives a good view of the site of the down platform, which was in the loop; the main road bridge and station are in the background. A single-coach unit, No 153318, approaches the station on 27 July 1992.

The second view is of the same location, but the view of the loop and station is blocked by trees. This is not a 'past' photograph, but was taken subsequent to the previous one on the occasion of the first steam train on the 'Tarka Line' since the 1960s. This took place on 2 May 1994 to celebrate 150 years of railways at Exeter. The engine is Class '4MT' No 80080, which was built by British Railways in 1954. *Both TG*

Above An equally attractive view is obtained from the bridge at the other end of the station, which forms part of a public footpath, accessible from a gate near the far end of the platform. The Ambrosia cream factory, which provided local employment and traffic for the railway, was located adjacent to the station. Built in 1928, it closed in 1970 and the buildings are now used for other purposes, most importantly as a fertiliser distribution depot. Until 1993 fertiliser was delivered by rail; deliveries were usually in the early hours of the morning one day a week or as requested. All fertiliser is now brought by road, thus depriving the 'Tarka Line' of its last freight facility. Other traffic included animals (live and dead) and coal, and there is still a coal merchant operating from the goods yard. The wagons seen on the right formed almost the last fertiliser train to use Lapford, and were taken away a few days after this photograph was taken. *TG*

SOUTHERN RAILWAY.

(3/25)

Stock 787

TO

LAPFORD

Author's collection

'Battle of Britain' Class No 34066 *Spitfire* passes through Lapford on a London-bound train in the early 1960s. Some 30 years later, single-car unit No 153362 enters the station forming a service from Barnstaple on 24 August 1993. *Lens of Sutton/TG*

An unmade road crosses the railway at Chenson and this also constitutes a public footpath. Both old and modern notices warn of the dangers of crossing the railway without attention. The small modern triangular sign on the right portrays an InterCity 125 train, which is not as incongruous at it may appear. Very occasionally an InterCity train is used for excursions from Barnstaple, for example to Hampton Court and to York.

The significance of Chenson is that this is the point where the south-east section of the Tarka Trail is first encountered. The Trail has run parallel to the River Taw from North Tawton and Bondleigh to just below Chenson. At Chenson, instead of crossing the railway, it remains on the west side of the line until Eggesford station is reached. *TG*

An excellent view of both the Tarka Trail (in the foreground) and the 'Tarka Line' can be had from Eggesford Garden Centre; similar views have been used in publicity material for the line. Cycles can be hired from the Garden Centre. The church is that of All Saints and was built for the benefit of the people of the Eggesford Estate. *TG*

Above With Eggesford Forest in the background, Class '150' No 150247 heads for Barnstaple on the 20 July 1992; the Tarka Trail lies to the left out of view. Eggesford Forest, much of which was once part of the Eggesford Estate whose history goes back to the 13th century, is owned by the Forestry Commission. There is a network of waymarked foot and cycle paths through the forest and several picnic areas. *TG*

Opposite page A reminder of the time when all trains were steam-hauled. 'West Country' Class No 34026 enters Eggesford on the 12.18 pm from Torrington to Waterloo on 3 August 1955.

Today Eggesford station is the only passing place for trains apart from Crediton. There is a level crossing at the station and the barriers are operated by the train crew, as the station is unstaffed. It is here also that the driver requires permission to proceed, and these two requirements usually result in a few minutes' wait at Eggesford, particularly if it is also necessary to pass a train heading in the opposite direction. Trains passing on 15 August 1987 are an Exeter-bound train hauled by Class '31' No 31406, seen from a northbound DMU. The main Exeter to Barnstaple road is immediately to the right

There is no village of Eggesford and the station is used by people from the nearby villages of Chawleigh and Chulmleigh and surrounding area. In the steam era there was a bus service to Torrington, but this ceased once private car ownership became commonplace. Amazingly, the service was reinstated in 1994 and one journey per week is made in each direction. *Denis Cullum/TG*

Author's collection

The telephoto lens gives a false sense of nearness of the church to Eggesford station. The position of the hut behind the 'Stop' sign was once occupied by a manually operated signal box. Built when the line was opened, the box was destroyed by flooding in the winter of 1967 and an ugly flat-roofed building replaced it until this was displaced in 1987 by the current means of controlling the barriers.

The second view shows present-day DMU No 150238 on an Exeter-bound service. *Both TG*

London and South Western Ry.
———
787
TO
EGGESFORD

Author's collection

Above The age of steam was also the age of oil lamps, and this relic survived at Eggesford until the early 1980s. The lamp post originally had an oil lamp attached permanently to the cast brackets, but this was later replaced by a rather unattractive pole, from which a Tilley lamp would be hung by the porter at dusk. *TG*

Above right It was also the age of passengers with large amounts of luggage, and porters to assist. This trolley was photographed at Eggesford in 1985, but placed behind bars out of reach of intending users. *TG*

Right Trains approach Eggesford from Barnstaple slowly both because of the tight curve and the warning signs, which apply in both directions. *TG*

The most famous landmark in the area was Eggesford House, built between 1820 and 1830 by the Hon Newton Fellowes, 4th Earl of Portsmouth. An earlier building of the same name located nearer the church was owned by the Copplestone family. Eggesford House remained with the Portsmouth family for three generations, and was sold by the 6th Earl in 1913. It then had a succession of owners, the last to occupy the house stripping it of much of the building material for use on his property elsewhere.

The house has remained in a state of dereliction ever since. In 1992 the Estate was sold and the present owners intend to restore part of the main house for their private use. *Beaford Archive/TG*

From Eggesford to Barnstaple the railway *is* the Tarka Trail, and for those visitors travelling from Exeter by train, this is an excellent introduction to the Trail. The intermediate stations, and particularly Umberleigh which has the better train service, are all good places to alight for a day's exploration of the surrounding countryside.

King's Nympton station is in one of the most attractive surroundings on the line and is located by a road junction known as Fortescue Cross. The station was originally named South Molton Road in an attempt to persuade travellers that the market town of the same name was close by; it was in fact 9 miles away. The GWR line to Barnstaple, which was opened much later, had its own station of South Molton only 1 mile from the town. Just after the nationalisation of the railways, South Molton Road was renamed King's Nympton after the nearest village 2½ miles away (and all uphill).

The first photograph shows Kings Nympton station, still with all its facilities, on 3 August 1955; the station buildings later passed into private ownership and today passengers are provided with a small bus-type waiting shelter. The hotel, which was advertised on the coach house roof, was recently closed. This was the Fortescue Arms, and Earl Fortescue had a say in the location of some of the stations on the line. *Denis Cullum/TG*

This really *is* the 1960s, unlike the photograph of the engine of the same class at Lapford on page 28. Two Class '4MT' engines, Nos 80039 and 80043, are on a special train from Torrington and Ilfracombe. This was the penultimate steam working on the line until 1994 and took place on 12 September 1965. A study of these photographs of King's Nympton (and those elsewhere in this book) shows the gradual reduction in facilities, from two platforms with signal box and passing loop, to a single line, one platform and no staff or booking facilities. *Ronald Lumber*

Left A closer view of the down starting signal, which even in the 1960s still retained the LSWR-style wooden post and arm. *TG*

London and South Western Ry.
787
From _____
TO
South Molton Road

Author's collection

Above and below left King's Nympton station from the main road bridge looking towards Exeter on 22 August 1986. Class '142' No 142022 forms the 08.30 from Exmouth, which called at all stations from Exeter except Newton St Cyres. By this time the passing loop had been removed and only one platform was in use.

The same place five years later shows more change with the addition of the waiting shelter and further encroachment of trees. This is unit No 828 formed from odd coaches from Classes '101' and '108' necessitated by the withdrawal of the new Class '142' railbuses. *Both TG*

Above right One of the King's Nympton's oil lamps amongst some trees in 1993. Most were sold in the 1960s for £4 10s 0d each, buyer collects! This included the lamp post itself on condition that the platform surface was made good following uprooting. Station names were etched on to the lamp glass (see page 24), but plain glass was fitted at King's Nympton at the time of the name change. *TG*

These two photographs of Station Road in King's Nympton village were taken about 70 years apart, yet only superficial changes have occurred. The shops on either side of the road (a general stores and boot-maker) have become private houses, and the view of the field is hidden by trees that have grown on the site of the building beyond the horses. There is also a school on the right just beyond the bottleneck. 'The Arms' notice hanging over the road may refer to the 'Fortescue Arms' at the bottom of the hill by the station. *Beaford Archive/TG*

Above Just north of King's Nympton the railway crosses the river at Junction Pool, to which reference is made in *Tarka the Otter*. This is the junction of the rivers Taw and Mole, the railway continuing to follow the former. The nearby King's Nympton Park Estate is owned by the Wildfowl Trust. *TG*

Right Between King's Nympton and the next station of Portsmouth Arms there are attractive views from the railway on both sides of the train. Good views of the railway are also plentiful, such as this one showing the 17.24 from Exeter St David's to Barnstaple on 18 August 1989. *TG*

Portsmouth Arms was another station without a village, and was named after the 4th Earl of Portsmouth of Eggesford House, under whose auspices the Exeter Road to Barnstaple was built. At several points on this road the old toll houses can still be seen.

Above **Portsmouth Arms station approach, with traditional telephone box and car, seen in the summer of 1986. The platforms are to the right behind the notice board and the main road on the far left.** *TG*

Below **An evening train (unit No 954) heading toward Exeter on 24 August 1989. The Station Master's house, now in private hands, is in the background.** *TG*

An Ilfracombe to Exeter train passes through Portsmouth Arms on a wet spring day in 1968 hauled by Class '42' 'Warship' locomotive No D812 *The Royal Naval Reserve 1859-1959*.

On 30 April 1994 the 08.24 Exmouth to Barnstaple train is the second of the day to stop at the much reduced station, formed of Class '150' No 150244. *Both TG*

Opposite A typical early 1960s train on the 'Tarka Line' is seen at Portsmouth Arms *en route* to Ilfracombe, hauled by 'Battle of Britain' Class No 34072 *257 Squadron*.

By 1966 the loop had been taken out and only the down platform was in use. The 17.45 Exeter Central to Ilfracombe passes through Portsmouth Arms on 28 May 1966. *Lens of Sutton/Ronald Lumber*

Above The present-day station is even more bare, with no signal box or main buildings. The old up platform is overgrown, but at least the station is still open as a request stop. At the time of writing there are two trains to Barnstaple and three in the other direction on weekdays. Modern lighting has replaced the oil lamps, one of which is now in the grounds of the nearby Portsmouth Arms public house. *TG*

London and South Western Ry.
——
787
TO
PORTSMOUTH ARMS

Author's collection

A little beyond Portsmouth Arms station on the Exeter Road is a staggered crossroads with byroads to the east and west. The surfacing of the road, modifications to the houses and growth of trees in the background does not prevent recognition of the present (1993) with the past (turn of the century) photographs. The view is looking towards Portsmouth Arms; the road to the left (out of sight beyond the houses) leads to a bridge over the railway line, from which there are excellent views towards Exeter. *Beaford Archive/TG*

Looking from that bridge on 21 August 1990, we see unit No 879 forming the 16.05 Exeter Central to Barnstaple train. *TG*

The adjacent field also gives a good view. On 29 April 1994 the train is worked by a Class '150' Sprinter.

The same location a few days *later* finds a steam train heading for Barnstaple. This is the outward working of the special train shown on page 28; the engine is Standard Class '4MT' No 80079. *Both TG*

Shortly before reaching Umberleigh the train slows down as it passes over a minor road. This is Umberleigh Gates, although the level crossing gates were removed in 1972 and the crossing is now open. On 22 August 1987 Class '33' No 33050 takes the 10.13 fast train (with two intermediate stops) to Exeter.

Much shorter trains are now the norm, represented by this 'Sprinter' working the 10.18 from Barnstaple to Exmouth on 30 April 1994. The crossing is located by the white house on the right. *Both TG*

This view overlooking Umberleigh, with the station in the background, was taken from a nearby hill in the early years of the railway.

The hill is now covered with trees, but a similar viewpoint can be obtained from behind the Rising Sun public house. Most of the buildings can still be recognised, although the station is partly obscured by the premises of Murch Bros, who deal in farming equipment which used to be delivered by rail. Both photographs show the road bridge over the River Taw in the foreground. *Beaford Archive/TG*

The original road bridge over the Taw was of narrow wooden construction and is seen here from the east bank, with the Rising Sun and the Exeter Road in the background.

The bridge was rebuilt during the First World War, but the view over the river has otherwise hardly changed. *Beaford Archive/TG*

DEVON COUNTY COUNCIL
UMBERLEIGH BRIDGE
REBUILT 1914-15

E. J. STEAD   COUNTY   C. POLLARD & SON
R. N. STONE   SURVEYORS   CONTRACTORS

Right The stone commemorating the rebuilding. *TG*

The Umberleigh to Barnstaple section of the line formed what was called the Taw Valley Extension, and was opened in 1854. Umberleigh is a most attractive station by virtue of a road overbridge at the northern end, giving a pleasant view of the station and countryside lying to the south, and from which these photographs were taken. Class '142' No 142019 pauses on its way to Barnstaple on 22 August 1986 (*opposite above*). Behind the train can be seen the sign imposing a speed restriction for Umberleigh Gates. In the right foreground is the remains of the short bay for the end loading of vehicles.

One of the locomotive-hauled trains brought in to substitute for a shortage of DMUs following the withdrawal of Class '142' units is seen at the same place in the summer of 1987 (*opposite below*). The engine is Class '33' No 33050.

In the third view (*above*) one of the latest generation of diesel units, Class '150' No 150244, leaves Umberleigh as the 16.05 from Exeter Central on 30 April 1994. *All TG*

Right The external views of Umberleigh, Morchard Road and Copplestone stations are very similar - this is Umberleigh in 1994. *TG*

Above Umberleigh was the only intermediate station between Crediton and Barnstaple to issue platform tickets in BR days. These were sought after by collectors as they were of pre-war SR origin. Ticket 0131 was issued on 10 December 1955. *Author's collection*

The wide arches of the bridge are evidence that the line was originally built to the broad gauge. The line was doubled from Umberleigh to Barnstaple in 1890, and this was the view in 1968.

The signal box was closed in 1971 when the line to Barnstaple was singled, and this 1994 view shows that it has now been demolished. Class '153' No 153302 has just made a brief stop on a late afternoon train from Exeter, from which three passengers alighted. *Both TG*

Right In common with the other stations on the line, Umberleigh had a goods yard with road access, guarded by a five-bar gate. The yard is now abandoned, and the gate, serving no useful function, is left permanently open and is gradually being hidden by encroaching natural growth. The Southern Railway recognised the attraction of the area for holiday makers and Umberleigh yard was one of several locations where Camping Coaches were available. *TG*

Below The railway bridge over the River Taw immediately after Umberleigh station can be seen from the road bridge over the river. Here a 'Sprinter' negotiates the bridge on 30 August 1993. *TG*

Contrasts on the line between Umberleigh and Chapelton. A Barnstaple-bound train is seen on 20 April 1992, then at the same location two years *later* is a steam train, which must have been something of a surprise to anyone walking down the path from which this photograph was taken! *Both TG*

Above Distances along the line were traditionally recorded from Waterloo at ¹/₄-mile intervals. Milepost 207 was immediately prior to reaching Chapelton, the last station before Barnstaple. *TG*

Below The green enamel nameboard at Chapelton was erected in Southern Railway days. The LSWR lamp post to the left has had its lamp removed. *TG*

Top Public access to Chapelton station is along a short unmade road also serving as a public footpath, which crosses the railway and the River Taw. *TG*

Above The comments about the then recently introduced open station system hardly apply at Chapelton. There is no ticket barrier and there are rarely more than two or three intending passengers. *TG*

Chapelton at the turn of the century, with the traditional line-up of staff for the photographer. The points in the foreground give access to a siding, in later years used to take timber from the adjacent sawmills, which are still in operation although there is no longer a siding here. The public footpath to the river can be seen in the foreground, and also gives access to the platform.

Only a few trains stop at Chapelton on weekdays. It is, however, in the unique position of having a Sunday service on only one occasion during the year, when all trains stop and there are more passengers than the total for a week. The reason for this activity is that the annual Chapelton steam fair is held nearby and the service is provided to encourage visitors to use the train, a commendable local initiative. One of these Sunday stopping trains pulls away from Chapelton on 27 August 1989 toward Barnstaple. The train is formed of two single-car units (Nos 103 and 105, both of Class '122') and two-coach unit No 955 (Class '108'). *Beaford Archive/TG*

The 'past' view is of Chapelton station in the 1970s. In contrast to other stations along the 'Tarka Line', when the track was singled it was not the platform with the main building that was retained; instead the down platform is used today, and the station house, which was on the up side, is now a private residence. *Both TG*

Two miles beyond Chapelton, at New Bridge, the Exeter Road crosses both the river and the railway before reaching the village of Bishop's Tawton. This is the approach to the village on the Exeter Road in the early 1900s, showing the parish church of St John the Baptist and the school immediately in front.

The main road was re-routed many years ago and the cottages are now spared the incessant noise and danger from modern-day through traffic. The main road can be seen at the foot of the hill passing left to right towards Barnstaple. New houses have been built opposite the cottages and the school, which was built in 1841, now serves as the village hall. The road past the cottages forms part of the north-east segment of the Tarka Trail from Barnstaple to Lynton. *Beaford Archive/TG*

For the remaining short journey to Barnstaple the scenery is far less interesting. The railway first crosses the River Taw yet again, then passes under the North Devon Link Road. Immediately thereafter on the right is the embankment of the line that once connected the GWR and LSWR systems; there is now a cycle and footpath along the old line.

The LSWR station of Barnstaple Junction, now referred to as plain Barnstaple, is situated on the western edge of the town, which is a short walk away over the impressive Taw Bridge. Barnstaple Junction was an important railhead, with two long platforms, a large goods yard, two signal boxes and an engine shed. In 1924 one of the platforms was converted into an island, thus increasing the capacity of the station to handle the summer holiday traffic.

Although it must be acknowledged that passenger traffic has fallen drastically since steam days, the provision of just one coach on some trains, particularly during the summer, is rather extreme and results in severe overcrowding, as seen in the photograph below.

Travelling hopefully, or, perhaps more to the point, hopefully travelling. Intending passengers for the return journey to Exeter await the arrival of single-coach Class '122' unit No 106, forming the 12.45 from Exmouth on 24 July 1992. Overcrowding seems inevitable. *Both TG*

This is Barnstaple Junction station in the early years of the Southern Railway, with Class 'X6' No 665 on an Exeter train. This engine was scrapped in 1933.

The 1962 view shows virtually no changes, other than the use of more modern motive power and rolling-stock. 'West Country' Class No 34023 *Blackmore Vale* stands in the same platform with an Ilfracombe to Exeter train on 21 April.

The same place on 16 August 1986. The train is the 16.00 all-stations (except Newton St Cyres) to Exeter hauled by Class '33' No 33211. This was one of only a few members of this class built with narrow bodies especially for the Hastings line, and it is not clear why it was so far from home territory. *Lens of Sutton/Terry Nicholls/TG*

Author's collection

The Ilfracombe portion of the down 'Atlantic Coast Express' approaches Barnstaple Junction (*above*) hauled by 'West Country' Class No 34011 *Tavistock* on 14 August 1963.

The last days of locomotive-hauled trains were imminent when this photograph (*above right*) was taken in August 1987. Class '31' No 31208 arrives on the Saturdays-only 15.48 from Exeter St David's. It was only on summer Saturdays that 1st Class accommodation was provided, and a study of the public timetable thus gave the clue as to which trains were scheduled to be locomotive-hauled and which were diesel multiple units.

What a contrast is this 1993 photograph (*right*), showing a two-coach train entering the station. The signal box ('A' box) has been demolished, all sidings have been removed and the centre island platform is falling into disrepair. Class '150' No 150240 arrives as the 14.15 from Exmouth on 30 August 1992. *P. Hutchinson/TG (2)*

London and South Western Ry.

787

From _____

TO

Barnstaple Junction

Author's collection

The signal box at the Exeter end of Barnstaple Junction a few months prior to closure. To the left is the turntable, and further to the left, out of sight, is the engine shed. *TG*

Above The interior of 'A' box was a good example of a traditional signal box where all operations were undertaken manually. It closed in November 1987, and shortly afterwards all semaphore signals were removed from the whole of the 'Tarka Line'. *TG*

Opposite Views of the station from the nearby road bridge also show that changes have taken place in relatively recent times. Class '42' No D805 *Benbow* has just arrived with the 08.10 from Paddington on 17 July 1971. Track alterations were taking place following closure of the line on to Ilfracombe, although the line in the foreground was still in use for freight trains to Torrington and beyond. Barnstaple's second signal box is just visible on the extreme left.

By 1987 there was no obvious trace of the junction for Ilfracombe, part of the land being taken over by Western Truck Rental. The goods yard had been closed in March and the track was in the process of being ripped up. Further changes have since taken place - there is now only one track and this terminates at the end of the main platform (see page 61). *Ronald Lumber/TG*

There was a bulk cement depot in the yard with a daily delivery. Class '31' No 31403 waits to leave for Exeter Riverside with the empty tanks on 27 August 1986. This service ceased the following year.

The second photograph shows the bleak view of the location today, with the Victorian terraced houses in the background. The station lies to the left. *Both TG*

The shed that housed engines for the heavy passenger and freight trains and the smaller engines for local services fell into disrepair in BR days and was without a roof by the time this photograph was taken. It formally closed in 1971 and was subsequently demolished, hardly a difficult task.

The whole area has since been cleared and part is now occupied by retail stores. There were plans for even more rationalisation (ie reduction of facilities), with a new basic station to be built a few yards closer to Exeter, but fortunately these have been abandoned. *R. C. Riley/TG*

No 142022, one of the Class '142' railbuses whose stay on the Barnstaple line was shortlived, leaves the station with the 12.40 service to Exeter on 17 August 1986.

The present-day scene finds Class '150' DMU No 150219 leaving a station now devoid of its sidings, signals and goods shed; the latter was demolished in 1995. *Both TG*

The signalman in Barnstaple West (or 'B') box has just collected the token from the crew of a train from Ilfracombe on 23 April 1962. The engine is 'West Country' Class No 34015 *Exmouth*.

In the second view Class '2MT' 2-6-2T No 41248 shunts the stock of the 14.40 from Torrington, while Type 2 diesel-hydraulic No D6328 waits for the Torrington portion of the 10.15 Waterloo to Ilfracombe train on 27 June 1964.

This was the site of the junction on 22 August 1987. The line to the left now only continued for a few hundred yards beyond the bridge, and after closure of the Torrington line was used to store rolling-stock and for running-round purposes. The locomotive is Class '31' No 31208.

Today the track has all gone, but in its place is the beginning of the Tarka Trail to Bideford and beyond forming the south-west segment of the Trail's 'figure eight'. *Terry Nicholls/Ronald Lumber/TG/TG*

COLEFORD JUNCTION
TO OKEHAMPTON
AND MELDON QUARRY

Two Class '33' locomotives have just passed the site of Coleford Junction (see page 23) on a train of empty wagons for Meldon on 12 August 1988. The bridge that can just be seen on the far left carries the 'Tarka Line'. *TG*

A cheap day return ticket from Exeter to Okehampton issued on 11 August 1960. *Author's collection*

Bow was the first station after Yeoford on the LSWR line over the edge of Dartmoor to Plymouth. Single-car unit No P116 enters the station with the 13.35 Exeter St David's to Okehampton service on 29 May 1972.

Bow station and goods yard are now both privately owned. Dartmoor Line trains do not call here or at the other two stations towards Okehampton. This is the view of the station in April 1998 loooking towards Exeter. *Ronald Lumber/TG*

Local trains originating from Exeter Central and two through trains per day from London stopped at North Tawton, but patronage was always light, the village being some distance to the north. 'Battle of Britain' Class No 34078 *222 Squadron* has just stopped with an Exeter to Padstow train.

The station buildings and goods yard are now in private hands, and the track has been singled and raised to platform level when the adjacent bridge over the road was raised to give clearance for heavy goods vehicles. *R. C. Riley/TG*

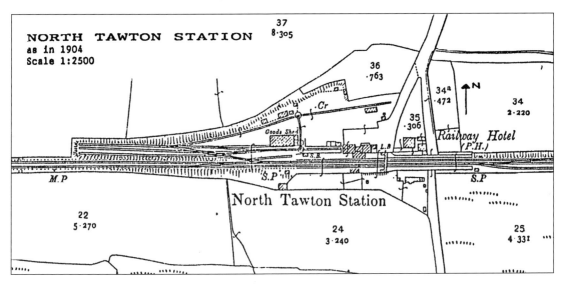

NORTH TAWTON STATION
as in 1904
Scale 1:2500

North Tawton Station

Above Plan of North Tawton station in 1904. *Courtesy Okehampton Museum of Dartmoor Life*

Below The imposing approach to North Tawton station. We meet the Tarka Trail again as it passes near the old station. *TG*

London and South Western Ry.

787

TO

North Tawton

Author's collection

After passing under the railway the Trail continues close to the River Taw, which skirts North Tawton town. Two large factories dominate North Tawton, one old and virtually abandoned and the other built only a few years ago. The former was a woollen mill; many of the original buildings seen in this early view were replaced, and these are now themselves mostly unused. The modern factory in the background belongs to Express Foods. The two views were taken from the nearby hill. The Trail continues north to meet the railway again at Chenson crossing (see page 31). *Beaford Archive/TG*

Little is left of Sampford Courtenay station other than the platforms and a small waiting shelter on the down side. On 25 May 1970 the 18.30 Okehampton to Exeter St David's service is worked by three-caoch DMU No LA309.

In the second photograph a Class '37' passes with a train-load of ballast *en route* to Exeter Riverside on 2 July 1993. *Ronald Lumber/TG*

Opposite Shortly before Okehampton, the train crosses Fartherford Viaduct, shown here in 1912. The viaduct is now virtually hidden from view by trees, but there are a few clearings between the railway and the bypass. The Tarka Trail passes almost under the viaduct. *Beaford Archive/TG*

The 1.00 pm from Waterloo to Plymouth climbs the last few yards into Okehampton on 11 August 1960 behind 'West Country' Class No 34106.

The line is now hemmed in by trees, and this is the same view on 27 July 1997. The train is the penultimate of the day to Exeter, formed of Class '150' No 150239. *Both TG*

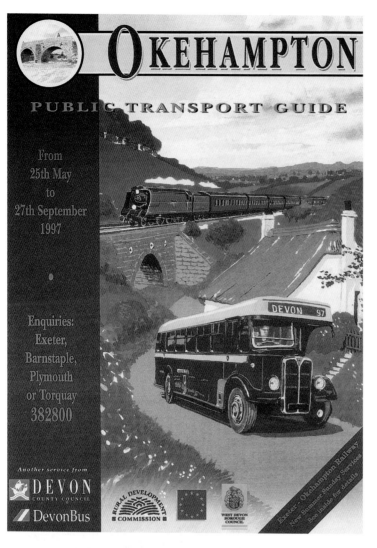

OKEHAMPTON

PUBLIC TRANSPORT GUIDE

From
25th May
to
27th September
1997

Enquiries:
Exeter,
Barnstaple,
Plymouth
or Torquay
382800

Another service from

DEVON
COUNTY COUNCIL

DevonBus

RURAL DEVELOPMENT
COMMISSION

WEST DEVON
BOROUGH
COUNCIL

DEVON 97

Exeter – Okehampton Railway
New Summer Sunday Services
See inside for details

Okehampton is well known for a number of reasons: to motorists it was one of the worst bottlenecks on the journey to Cornwall from the Home Counties, as the A30 trunk road passed through the centre of the town. Okehampton is also on the edge of Dartmoor, whose less attractive attributes are a military training area and Meldon Quarry, the latter providing ballast for the railways since its opening in 1897. In the town centre is the excellent Museum of Dartmoor Life, with much to interest the industrial archaeologist and the naturalist.

Left **The Summer 1997 Okehampton Pulic Transport Guide** *Reproduced by courtesy of Devon County Council*

Opposite **Okehampton was the interchange point for the Plymouth and North Cornwall lines, with some trains dividing here. It was very busy with both passenger and freight traffic, and even had its own small engine shed. The present station was built by the Southern Railway, and this 'past' view shows the original LSWR station. Note that the footbridge was not replaced during the rebuilding, but the new signal box is in a different place from the original.**

A mixed train consisting of one coach and several 'Walrus' and other ballast wagons enters the station on 11 August 1960 hauled by Class 'T9' No 30313. A passenger service was provided exclusively for quarrymen and their families between Meldon Halt and Okehampton. *Beaford Archive/TG*

BRITISH RAILWAYS (W)   S.1

OKEHAMPTON

PLATFORM TICKET 1d.
Available ONE HOUR on DAY OF ISSUE ONLY
NOT VALID IN TRAINS. NOT TRANSFERABLE
To be given up when leaving Platform
FOR CONDITIONS SEE BACK

1 | 2 | 3 | 4 | 5 | 6

Both author's collection

London and South Western Ry.
787
TO
Okehampton

A DMU service was operated from Exeter to Okehampton from 1968 to 1972, but all other passenger services beyond Okehampton were withdrawn in the former year, except those between Bere Alston and Plymouth. This line still enjoys a service, which continues to Gunnislake on the Cornish side of the River Tamar. Even after 1972 Okehampton saw occasional passenger trains, bringing walkers and other visitors. In the summer of 1986 there were two passenger trains on each of several Saturdays, and the extremely rare event of Class '142' railbuses in the station was recorded on 23 August; the units are Nos 142019 and 142026.

On weekdays, Meldon Quarry trains still rumble through Okehampton, although plenty of time and patience is needed, as they rarely run on time and are very often early, very late or cancelled. Here Class '33' Nos 33039 and 33064 pass through the station on their way to Exeter Riverside on 17 August 1988. *Both TG*

Above Posters advertising the 1986 summer services. The trains were poorly patronised and no similar services were run until 1997, when the response was overwhelming. *TG*

Below On 25 May 1997, prior to the re-instatement of passenger services, a special train conveying invited guests, including railway, quarry, county and local authority officials, was run from Exeter St David's to Okehampton. It was worked by a Class '37' locomotive at each end; No 37415 is seen here at the Exeter end of the train. *TG*

'West Country' Class No 34106 *Lydford* heads the 1.00 pm Waterloo to Plymouth train, while Class 'T9' No 30313 waits for connecting passengers before leaving with the 5.51 pm all-stations service to Halwill Junction and Wadebridge on 11 August 1960. The London train has split at Exeter Central, the rear portion being for Ilfracombe, where it is due to arrive at 7.02 pm.

During the period that Okehampton station was closed, it became more and more decrepit, with the edges of the platforms crumbling away and the footbridge being unsafe. The second view shows the station in 1993. *Both TG*

Another view of the 'T9' at the head of the 5.51 pm departure from Okehampton on 11 August 1960. The 'present' view shows that after years of neglect the station has been restored to a good state of repair and decoration in preparation for the new summer weekend services. This is the last train of the day to Exeter on 27 July 1997, formed by Class '150' No 150248. The goods shed on the right is now a youth hostel. *Both TG*

Immediately at the Exeter end of the station was a small engine shed complete with coaling and turning facilities. Another 'T9', No 30717, is receiving attention on 11 August 1960.

In this summer 1997 view the remnants of these facilities can still be seen, despite the area now being given over to car parking for railway passengers. The site of the turntable is easily located in what is now a road. *Both TG*

Okehampton town centre is dominated by the church, and this is the main road (Fore Street) long before the days of the motor car and its upgrading to form part of the A30.

All the buildings still exist today, although most are now put to different uses. The virtual absence of traffic demonstrates that the photograph was taken after the opening of the Okehampton bypass in 1988. This location is at the intersection of the main road with the road from Hatherleigh to the left, and that to Okehampton station and the moor to the right. The station is high above the town and the railway line clings to the edge of Dartmoor from here to Tavistock. *Beaford Archive/TG*

Above There was little access to the railway between Okehampton and Meldon. Class 'T9' No 30717 works the 3.15 pm from Bude on this isolated stretch of line in the summer of 1960. *TG*

Below The building of the Okehampton bypass has given new opportunities to see the railway in the vicinity of Okehampton. On 14 August 1991 two Class '33s', Nos 33002 and 33208, descend from Meldon Quarry toward Okehampton. The bypass can be seen in the left background. *TG*

Meldon Quarry on 7 July 1961: a Class 'G6' had been allocated here for shunting for many years. This is No DS 682, which was later displaced by a Class 'USA' tank. When steam was withdrawn a Class '08' took over the shunting duties, as seen in the second view. *Both TG*

A visit to Meldon Quarry on 22 August 1990 witnessed much activity, with the arrival and departure of several stone trains and movement of wagons within the quarry yard. The resident shunter was Class '08' No 08584, and the engine taking stone to Exeter Riverside was Class '50' No 50015. *Both TG*

An up stone train in the hands of a Class 'N' locomotive leaves the quarry on 7 July 1961. The halt for quarry employees was located just to the left of this location.

Two Class '37' locomotives meet on the occasion of the centenary of the opening of Meldon Quarry in 1997. No 37667 brings the special celebration train past a train of hoppers hauled by No 37694. *Both TG*

A 'West Country' Class 'Pacific' crosses Meldon Viaduct with the 11.00 am Plymouth to Portsmouth train on 7 July 1961. The viaduct remained out of use for many years, but was invaded by visitors on 24 May 1997 as part of the centenary celebrations. It will see many more visitors in the future, as it is being opened as part of a new cycleway. *Both TG*

BIBLIOGRAPHY

Transport

Around the Branch Lines, Volume 1, Terry Gough (Oxford Publishing Company, 1982)
    ISBN 86093 159 5
British Railways Past and Present: Devon, David Mitchell (Past & Present, 1991)
The Tarka Trail: A Past and Present Companion, Terry Gough (Past & Present, 1998)
British Roads Past and Present: Devon, Valerie R. Belsey (Past & Present, 1993)
    ISBN 1 85895 0007
Cross Country Routes of the Southern, Terry Gough (Oxford Publishing Company, 1983)
    ISBN 0 86093 267 2
Devon and Cornwall Railways in Old Photographs, Kevin Robertson (Alan Sutton, 1989)
    ISBN 0 86299 667 8
Exeter to Barnstaple, Vic Mitchell and Keith Smith (Middleton Press, 1993) ISBN 1 873793 1 5 4
The Kingdom by the Sea, Paul Theroux (Penguin, 1984) ISBN 0 14 007181 4
LSWR West Country Lines Then and Now, Mac Hawkins (David & Charles, 1993)
    ISBN 0 7153 0122 5
The North Devon Line, John Nicholas (Oxford Publishing Company, 1992) ISBN 0 86093 461 6
Railway World Special - The Southern West of Exeter, Peter Semmens (Ian Allan, 1988)
    ISBN 0 7110 1806 5
A Regional History of the Railways of Great Britain, Volume I: The West Country,
    David St John Thomas (David & Charles, 1981) ISBN 0 7153 8210 1
The Southern West of Salisbury, Terry Gough (Oxford Publishing Company, 1984)
    ISBN 0 86093 341 5
The Withered Arm, T. W. E. Roche (Forge Books, 1977)

Ordnance Survey Maps

First Edition (approx 1880): sheets 74, 82, reprinted by David and Charles, 1970
Popular Edition (approx 1918): sheets 118, 127, 128, 137
New Popular Edition (approx 1940): sheets 163, 175, 176
Landranger Series (current): sheets 180, 191

Town and Country

Barnstaple and North West Devon (Fifteenth Edition, Ward Lock, 1952)
Barnstaple, Town on the Taw, Lois Lamplugh (Phillimore, 1983)
Barnstaple Yesterday, Julia Barnes and Jonathan Baxter (Robert and Young, 1992)
Changing Devon, James Derounian, Chris Smith and Chris Chapman (Tabb House Ltd, 1988)
Devon Town Trails, Peter Hunt and Marilyn Wills (Devon Books, 1988)
Exploring Barnstaple, John Bradbeer (Thematic Books, 1990) ISBN 0 948444 177
Market Towns of North Devon, Rosemary Anne Lauder (Badger Books, 1983) ISBN 0 946290 04 0
North Devon Country in Old Photographs (Parts I and II), Beryl Yates (Alan Sutton, 1989)
    ISBNs 0 86299 652X, 0 86299 727 5
Postcard Views of North Devon, Volume I (Ilfracombe), Volume II (Barnstaple),
    Volume III (South Molton), Tom Bartlett (Badger Books)
A Tale of Two Rivers, Rosemary Anne Lauder (1985) ISBN 0 946 290 11 3
Tarka Country, Trevor Beer (Badger Books, 1983) ISBN 0 946 290 059
The Tarka Trail, A Walker's Guide, produced by the Tarka Project (Devon Books, 5th ed, 1998)
    ISBN 0 86114 8770 0
Vanished Houses of North Devon, Rosemary Anne Lauder (North Devon Books, 1981)
    ISBN 0 9507920 04
A Visitor's Guide to Devon, Brian Le Messurier (Moorland Publishing, 1983)

Further information on Tarka Country and the Tarka Line is available from the Tarka Country Tourism
Association, 01271 345008.

INDEX OF LOCATIONS

Barnstaple Junction 61-73
Bishop's Tawton village 60
Bow 75

Chapelton 56-59
Chenson Crossing 31
Coleford Junction 74
Copplestone 23-25
Cowley Bridge Junction 16
Crediton 18-19

Eggesford 31-35
　Eggesford House 36
Exeter Central 10-13
Exeter St David's 14-15

King's Nympton 6, 37-39
　Junction Pool 41
　village 40

Lapford 28-30

Meldon Quarry 90-93
　Viaduct 94
Morchard Road 26-27

Newton St Cyres 17
North Tawton 76-77
　village 78

Okehampton 81-88
　Fartherford Viaduct 80
　town 89

Portsmouth Arms 42-45
　Exeter Road 46-48

Sampford Courtenay 79

Umberleigh 50, 52-55
　Gates 49
　village 50-51

Yeoford 20-22